THE CHRISTMAS STORY

Based on the Gospels according to Saint Matthew and Saint Luke

Retold by Deborah Hautzig
Illustrated by Tony Chen

HAPPY HOUSE BOOKS
Random House, Inc.

Text originally published by Random House, Inc., in 1981.

Text copyright © 1981 by Random House, Inc. Illustrations copyright © 1987 by Tony Chen. All rights reserved under International and Pan-American Copyright Conventions. Published in the United States by Random House, Inc., New York, and simultaneously in Canada by Random House of Canada Limited, Toronto. ISBN: 0-394-88582-1 Manufactured in the United States of America   2 3 4 5 6 7 8 9 0

Long ago in the city of Nazareth there lived a
carpenter named Joseph and his wife, Mary.
They had a small house, and they had a donkey,
but they did not have any children.

One day, when Mary was alone in the garden,
an angel appeared. It was the angel Gabriel.
Mary did not know why Gabriel had come, and
she was afraid.

"Do not be afraid, Mary," the angel said. "You are special and favored by God, and he has chosen you to be the mother of his son. Your son's name will be Jesus. He will be born a king and his kingdom will never end."

Mary was very happy.

When it was almost time for Mary to have her baby, Joseph said, "We must take a trip to Bethlehem to pay our taxes. It is a long journey, but you can ride our donkey." And so they went.

When Mary and Joseph came to Bethlehem,
it was late at night and they were very tired.
But there was no room for them at the inn.
The innkeeper said they could sleep in the stable,
so they went there to rest for the night.

In the stable were a cow, a lamb, a goat, and a
dove. The animals were friendly. They let Joseph
and Mary use their hay for a bed.

That very night, Mary's child was born. She
wrapped him in soft cloth to keep him warm.
There was no crib for the baby, so Mary laid
him in the animals' manger.

In the fields outside of Bethlehem, shepherds watched over their flocks of sheep. Suddenly a light appeared in the night sky. The shepherds looked up and saw an angel. They were afraid until the angel spoke.

"I am bringing you news of great joy," said
the angel. "Tonight in the city of Bethlehem,
a savior has been born. He is called Jesus Christ,
and he is our Lord. You will find the baby
wrapped in swaddling clothes, lying in a manger."

The shepherds went to Bethlehem. When they
found the stable, they were filled with joy at the
sight of the child and knelt beside the manger to
honor him. Then they went out to tell people
what the angel had said about the newborn baby.

Far away in the east lived three wise men named Caspar, Melchior, and Balthazar, who had watched the skies for many years. They knew that someday a new star would rise to announce the birth of their king.

At last it appeared—a bright, glowing star
they had never seen before.

The wise men set out to follow the star. They
traveled westward across many miles of desert.
The star was their guide. It led them to Bethlehem.
Then it came to rest right above the little stable.

The wise men entered the stable, and when they saw the baby they knew they had found their king.

They gave him gifts of gold and wonderfully scented perfumes, frankincense and myrrh.

The wise men worshiped the child as the shepherds had, and they rejoiced.

Even the animals in the stable knew how special this baby was. Everyone knew he would be kind and gentle. They knew he would be a wise teacher, and a friend to all animals and to all people.

And he was. Every year at Christmastime, we celebrate the birth of Jesus Christ, because he brought the good news of God's love to all living things.